THOMAS CRANE PUBLIC LIBRARY

QUINCY MASS

CITY APPROPRIATION